Balboa Press books may be ordered through booksellers or by contacting:

Balboa Press
A Division of Hay House
1663 Liberty Drive
Bloomington, IN 47403
www.balboapress.com
1 (877) 407-4847

Because of the dynamic nature of the Internet, any web addresses or links contained in this book may have changed since publication and may no longer be valid. The views expressed in this work are solely those of the author and do not necessarily reflect the views of the publisher, and the publisher hereby disclaims any responsibility for them.

Any people depicted in stock imagery provided by Getty Images are models, and such images are being used for illustrative purposes only.
Certain stock imagery © Getty Images.

ISBN: 978-1-9822-2837-8 (sc)
ISBN: 978-1-9822-2838-5 (e)

Library of Congress Control Number: 2019906637

Print information available on the last page.

Balboa Press rev. date: 06/06/2019

BALBOA.
PRESS
A DIVISION OF HAY HOUSE

To my Family and Friends with thankfulness

Contents

Foreword

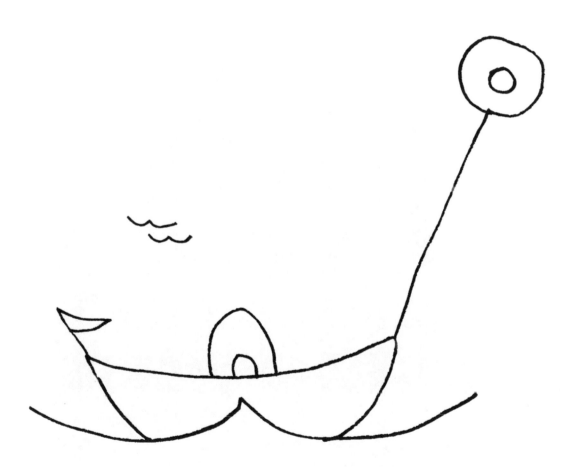

HAP

Hap's Donut Boat has a dragon watching over it.

As a child she always sensed an angel, or an ancestor or a nature guide around her, Hap decided it was a dragon! The dragon has lived in the river valley since then with her, as her Spirit Guide. The dragon always brings play, and excitement and a blissful mood. Hap sees her dragon in the morning mist and fog, in the sunset sky, in the clouds, and very often in the movement of the waves in the changing light and breeze.

A long time ago she began to keep her sketchbook to draw her dragon images as it appeared to her. Hap writes to describe her feelings. Her journals and drawing books have become many by now. Her poetry reflects the fun of the changing sky and water and the turtles and birds and rocks and trees and flowers she finds herself among each day.

Hap has a happy word for everyone she meets along the way up and down the river, as well as sparkling eyes and a friendly smile. One day pushing off from shore after supplying some of her regular campers firewood and water, a child shouted out to her "Hey Hap! See you later!" and the name Hap begin to echo all through the valley when seeing the Donut Boat coming.

Growing flowers was in her ancestry. Today many wildflowers in the river valley where once seeds she scattered. The rivers edge and shoreline is now colorful and yes, Happy! Fresh lemon and rosemary donuts that Miss. Lemon bakes get handed out on every stop on full and new moons.

Haps dragon poem…

"Eagle is in flight often indicate he's near, eagle in the tree indicate he is here. And in the bright colors of the sunset sky I see my dragon's eye!"

A Simple Introduction to some Colorful Characters

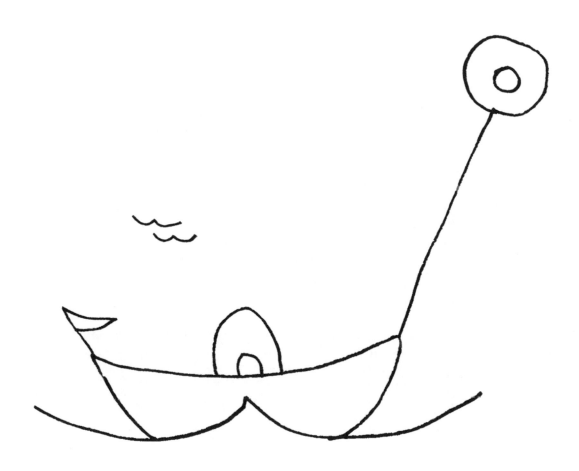

This is a story about Hap and Shiny and their friends they call family.

Shiny tends the horses and Hap floats the boat! The Donut Boat supplies donuts, hot coffee and firewood to the campers along the banks of the river.

This day the clouds move out after the night storm and the sweet sunlight breaks through. The air is heavy and misty along the river bed. Everyone wants to see the big inflated donut tethered high above the Donut Boat coming their way today. Excitement grows at the first sight as it comes around the point. Good morning smiles to and from all. Campfires start to blaze.

The ponies all get a little sweet feed and a flake of hay from Shiny to start the day, and an ear rub. Soaking in the sunlight after the storm, steam lifts from the horses coats; as the fiddler plays the morning song.

Hap heads down river to the camp of Pluto and Mim, with supplies for the week. Pluto reads horoscopes on the beach, while Mim plays her clay finger flute and tambourine for all that pass by their camp. The beautifully painted purple and blue wagons in their camp are easy to spot. Many dogs laying in the sun or playing about. The coffee is always hot on the fire. Mim sells colorful scarves and wooden animal totems that Pluto has carved. She wears layers of shawls and he has a maroon scarf around his waist. She has deep colored eyes with fire burning inside them and he has eyes of blue, blue, sweet light blue.

Pluto sees everywhere the sacred geometry; the spiral of the shell and the pattern of the pineapple. He loves to calculate the movement of the planets. A master cabinet maker; there will always be secret door or drawer built-in.

When I first met Mim she lived in the high hills west of here and kept a small house boat in the bay. With her love for nature and the study of ancient wisdom; a multi layered love for life radiates across her face!

Coming to shore Hap sees the smiles on their faces!

The orange ball of the sun dropped from the sky. In the after colors of the sunset one last plane is coming in low along the horizon. The sliver moon has grown a bit, the fire starts up, and a sweet guitar solo. A spotted line in the twilight sky is the geese heading out.

It's been a calm sunny day deep in November. From the porch the blue and white and little yellow planes circle around – must be take off and landing practice today, in the near field past the pines. Then a beautiful silver and red one commands the sky; it's Don giving us I flyby.

Most of the river boats are off of the water by now. Hap plans to take her boat out one more time – next Sunday. When Hap comes in we all pull her boat out of the river for the season. There is always a small parade and a feast that day. Shiny, bareback on his stallion, always leads the parade.

The river opened early, eagles eating fish on the last ice slabs. Robins return, and the frogs wake up in the pond.

Each spring the Donut Boat is pulled from the barn with a fresh coat of paint, beautifully detailed. We all jump on and pose for pictures… So much fun and gladness we have!

Soon after the Donut Boat gets in the water Hap and Shiny get together with some of their friends, and nieces and nephews. When the high water of spring goes down they take time to clean up the debris from the islands and shores on the upper river. It is a fun and work filled few days.

Shiny will bring his horses back to the river camp when the ground dries up a bit. They winter at his cabin nearby. The river land was a gift from Shiny's great uncle, it had been a loggers camp. It is made up of a scattering of shabby structures that he works to restore and preserve.

This is where the gathering of friendship and poetry happens each year.

Over the long winter everyone writes poetry, and creates art to bring their best to share in the meadow gathering. Hap and Shiny arrange everything from dry straw bales in a circle, the fire, the ribbons, and the cookies and tea. We dress up! Don always gives us a fly-by. The horses are tethered around, and nibble on a fresh green patch. Oh yes, there is music and a singing bowl!

Shiny's good friend, Buddy comes for the summer. His sisters May May, an artist, and Sweetness, a performing artist come with their mother for the poetry gathering.

Haps mom is wildly fun and raises companion chickens just downstream. Hap lives in her barn, where she winters the Donut Boat. Her sister and family come out from the southwest each summer.

Most everyone brings a relative or apprentice with them to the poetry gathering; for the purpose of teaching and sharing the experience. Shiny brings his nephew Makwa. He loves the atmosphere, the horses, and is a colorful poet himself. Last year his poems were about the Hepatica blooming purple on top of Eagle Mountain, and the sunbathing turtles on the river rocks. Makwa is gentle, smart and willing. Makwa's best friend Will comes to the gathering from upriver with his mentor, Curly Willow. Curly Willow is a well received elder in the valley, with a cheerful spirit, and a curious imagination. Whenever there is lightning in the sky it usually accumulates over his cabin on Eagle Mountain! Will is bird watching up there this summer.

Miss Lemon lives up river and she bakes all the goodies. She also brings her best friend Cookie.

A fun couple comes out and teaches log rolling at the nearby beach, and most often joins in.

That must be the loudest tree frog in the Universe! Sure to be signaling the gathering heard far and wide.

The gathering morning starts early; it's a big day, the rooster is crowing. Shiny is busy brushing out the muddy horses. Pluto and Mim are coming from the North Shore with their new house boat and should arrive by mid-morning. The campfire start up and the breakfast smells good. Celebrating is in everyone's atmosphere, gladness inside and out and there is a flute. The flags are flying and someone is chopping wood. Breathe it all in!

Eldon picks up Irma from the island and flies her in. Everybody feels especially excited to see her arrive. Shiny's beautiful bay mare pulls the wagon out to the field with happy children and dogs following behind. The children hold their colorful ribbons high and run, birds are flying and the drum beats faster and faster. Shiny drives the wagon in a circle around the meadow and onto the encampment for all to greet Irma eye to eye.

Many are flying in for today. Small planes circling around overhead, and others are lined up in the field.

The party doesn't start until everyone is here.

We all gather in the highest part of the meadow. A day like this goes on forever and ever and ever.

Mim and Pluto started the poetry reading tradition and always start us off. Wow! They look so great; colors and light just spinning around them! Mim opens with a sweet finger flute song and speaks the first poem of the day.

"Fancy a soft cloud and have a good night sleep.
When you are down, think up and when
you are up think upper!"

That is a surprise, as her poems so often rhyme.

There has been talk about putting them all together in a little book to share.

And they did...

Do you know?

You can be face to face with your spiritual master right now!
Do you want to?
Do you know how good it feels?
Do you know how fun it is?
It's good to be good, it's fun to be fun!

You don't have to fall off your donkey... Though some do!

All that is, is free; cross the bridge daily.

The little forest should always be kept clean and the fairies will dance and sing.

THE CALL of the GATHERING

Never flown in a hot air balloon
or slept much past noon
or had my own silver spoon
or doubted that the change would come soon;
but I've tasted the green cheese
and met the Man in the Moon!

On every walk in every woods I fall in love with something new.
Finding lots of leaves and the seasons each turn.
Roots and moss, and spiderweb lace, elves and fairies and a friends face.

If we could live the way we love,
we would live forever;
and we will!

A poem for Maybell

All the different flowers in the one garden.
All the different colors in the one garden.
Some spread, some reach, some creep,
some bloomed yesterday, some bloom today, some bloom tomorrow;
all thriving all striving in the one garden.

Breathing the Bridge

From the deepest sweet sleep you woke me... Up now, stretching,
I can feel you in my bones.

The sounds of singing and the taste of coconut coffee.

I am here with the smiling forehead, breathing deeply in and out.
From the center of this world to the highest heavens and back again making
the bridge with my breath. Both are both the inhale and the exhale are both
the world and the heavens changing back and forth.

Standing with one foot in each ocean I am the bridge,
a stitch in the seam of the fabric, you are the thread.

That's who I am. That's what I'm doing here!

Tie your camel here; where the two oceans meet and throw your 7000 seeds into the sea.

Be a greeter at the garden gate with me.

The sense of joy returns again to life.
Joyfully we dedicate our life to opening the way.
I know the gardener and the fountain builder I know the jeweler and I've placed some stepping stones and I know you.

And that's good for a good laugh!

We are made out of Stardust and now we shine!

Blue is my truck

I only say my - for no one else will.
I'll sit here and sing and dance and be free, until the energies right
she'll start, you'll see!

99 Steps to the Beach

99 steps to the beach,
bare feet moving towards happiness,
belonging on this quest to refresh.
The little road turns to green grass draws me,
101 steps and IN!

The butterfly

Now she can fly and her life is new,
perhaps for tea she'll come to visit with you.
When the sun is high and the sky is blue.
Keep this our secret and your dreams will come true.
The a butterfly will bring a gift to you.

Three magic words...
The secret of birds...
Blessing you with wings too!

When my part was that of the fool I learned to break every rule.

Like Humpty Dumpty I had a great fall
everyone was deaf to my helpless call.

Moving on...

Losing the fool in the white rabbit hall, though the jokers part was small, what I didn't dream up I could recall.

Then nothing happened at all.

My body recognized the end of the fall.

My lasting dream to some day walk tall
and dance in time above the wall,
and come when the angels call.

By then the joker was left behind.

The rainbows and some hoped to find.

And I had gone away, to sit on a cloud one whole day with nothing to say was my dream come true;

to kiss the sun go by and make love to the blue!

What is your dream come true?

Is it for one or is it for two?

Have you made love to the blue?

I painted my pony
and we livened up the parade!
Excited and alive, high stepping his prance,
his beauty reflected on the faces of everyone who saw him.

Take care!
to grab your Stetson and put it on,
when the wind comes up with a chill in the air.

The greetings while wearing a big nose, big smiles, and big shoes.
Seems like the handshakes never end.
When it's a parade I am in it!
We are in it!
Waving and walking by in front of the bagpipe band and drummers.
Home for a clown is in the kids parade with the fairy princesses and the
super heroes on the dirt path around camp!

We Laughed

Mom didn't want to die
for the longest time.
We had so much fun
With whatever we did towards the end.
When there was not much left to do
we remembered and relived all the good times.
Even if they really weren't so good.
We recalled and embellished the stories with laughter.

Our mining claims in New Mexico,
In the fall of 79' when gold and silver prices skyrocketed.
There we were staking our claims, together.
Mom dared to have fun.
Separately, we took the road less traveled and found each other there.
We loved each other to the core!
We didn't always like each other so well.
We were each other's teacher.
We could always count on each other.
And there was always a lot we needed from each other.

She was going to die first.
And I was going to let her go.
What a huge undertaking!
The biggest. The most important!
We took all the time we could to get it right.
It had to be right! We had to know it was.

It was the greatest thing we ever did,
and we are so grateful to be given the opportunity!

The lake accepted us with gladness.

The sky and the sun danced us into deep breaths of appreciation.

There were only words like bliss, love, enjoy... All denseness disappeared.

We trusted each twilight enthusiastically, and we are all different now.

We are in acceptance that we are.

Our energy base is a little higher.

We acknowledge this gift with enjoyment.

We got it – we wanted it –

and with it came the gift of the First Kiss Apple straight from the orchard.

We wanted to share everything with you.

Water... Waves... And reflections shine.

Come on take a ride on my chariot anytime.

Yes, I clean up myself every day and night.

I rake up my leaves and debris from my driveway.

Try to understand,

I pray to the Gods and Goddesses to enter my home,

and give blessings to my family.

I surely prepare the entrance!

The lovers and leavers of young and of all, and there once in a lifetime stories they've told.

Fallen leaves and befriended thieves, invisible seas, grandfather trees.

And in learning to believe my ideas are conceived and my heart relieved.

At times I'm alone and in the sun my hair is hot.

I've learned lessons of losing from the passerby.

Only some like you do I meet Eye to Eye.

Imagining and cultivating our hearts desire; we spin the world with our fastest six white horses. Moving life beyond what it has been before.

I walk among the woods in the grasses, along the creek and contemplate.

I marvel at the look of the river as the sunlight crosses the water.

I am beyond content.

I saw at Angel give a turkey leg to a hungry man and because I look I see that Angel every day.

Putting tobacco down is a way I learned.

Super moon shining on me puts a new light on you.

The night light bright as can be.

Woke up late today all the birds did too.

Feeling like there is more love today.

Like the heart of the whole world is bigger and brighter now.

Open... Brilliant... And happy!

Everything is changed a bit.

Heading out to fill the feeders, build a fire, and talk to the birds about it.

The birds always takes center stage.

The loon in the lake.

Morning dove looking out from her birdbath perch.

The cardinal all red and welcome.

The woodpecker on the curly willow.

The pheasant under the feeder.

The cranes are wearing their red ribbons.

This is happy!

I saw my Beloved on the path ahead.
I reached for him,
and he hopped away!

Who will say the last goodbye when the mountain takes to the sky,
and that tree becomes the sea.
So now that you know, please let me, go, alone and say my last goodbye.
My heart is heavy and longs to be free and he with the power can have me to
become the sea.
How will we be ready and how we cope with the love with the knowing.
Yes, you Magic Mountain is why I come back
to love and to know and to grow.
So dear mountain of mine before you must go,
tell me the secret that you know.

Feed the birds and plant the flowers seeds

Closing of the Gathering

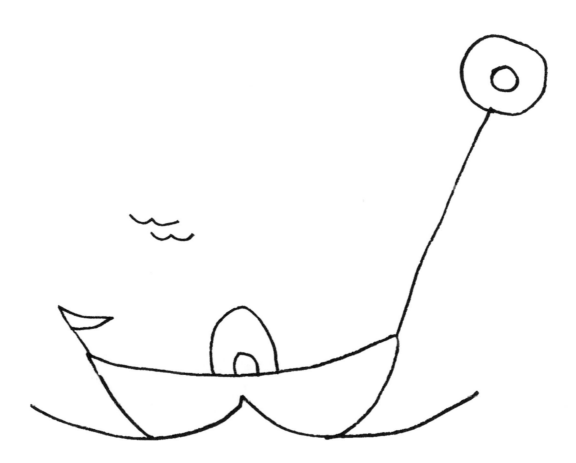

We gathered at sun down on the river bank; the fire burned deep into the night to fiddlers playing.

Until we meet again, carry on dear friends.

Wisdom

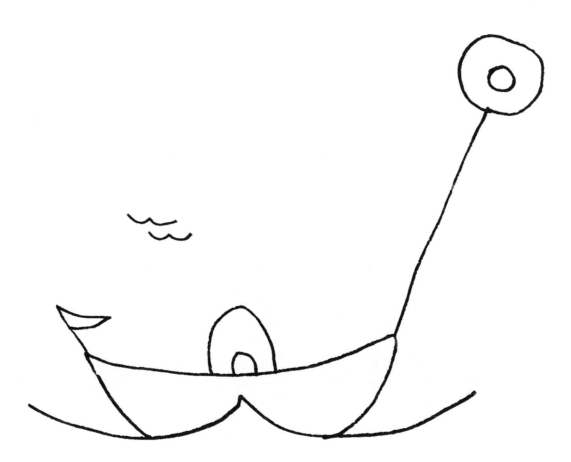

Simply simplify.
Start to practice, clear your mind, calm the chatter.
Relax, round off the rough edges of the feelings in your heart.

Imagining I am the donut boat.
It is my imaginations intent and persistence and love that moves my focus to clarity.
I set my compass and head down stream to my desire and amazement and delight!

There is much passion swirling together in this electric, magnetic stuff that moves us, hold us and lights us up.
We surrender and step off the edge of our separate outside self and dive freely in.
And fly with the birds in the sky!

The donut boat is your imagination, your fancy, your dream, your treasure!
Quiet your mind, and relax into your imagination.
What clicks inside us when we burst into laughter?
And when we all burst into laughter together?
What magic is released?
10,000 flowers! 10,000 birds!
Imagine the excitement!
This is your happy place!
This is where you thrive!
In the movement of the water, the jumping of the fire.

When you want something, intend for it to be and imagine it right here now!
The Donut Boat will cross the cosmic soup of your intention and bring it right to you!
Take your wanting, hoping, believing all the way up to knowing!

It's your imagination the Universe wants to play with!

Be there when the crack of sunlight comes over your neighbors home and shine back at it.

Be there with a heartfelt smile inside and give it to this day, so freely and thankful.

Be brilliant!

Unteather all thoughts and take flight.

Put on your HAPPY HAT!

Get involved.....and lose yourself today.

Enjoy a lemon rosemary donut with coffee or tea.

Your own personal Donut Boat has just arrived!

Come play with me!!!

Printed in the United States
By Bookmasters